ON LOVE
AND LOSS

ON LOVE AND LOSS

STEVEN KING

CALL OF CROWS

First published in Great Britain in 2021
by Call of Crows
Lyddington
Rutland

Printed and bound by Hobbs the Printers Ltd
Cover and text design by University of Hertfordshire Press
Cover image: A clay-backed face. Roman votive offering.
Credit: Wellcome Collection. CC BY 4.0

© Steven King 2021
All rights are reserved and remain with the author.

Steven King is hereby identified as author of this work in accordance with Section 77 of the Copyright Designs and Patents Act 1988. No reproduction, copy or transmission of any part of this publication may be made without written permission except in accordance with the Copyright Designs and Patents Act 1988, or under the terms of any licence permitting limited photocopying issued by the Copyright Licensing Agency, Barnards Inn, 86 Fetter Lane, London EC4A 1EN.

Any person undertaking or facilitating unauthorised copying may be liable to criminal prosecution and civil claims for damages.

ISBN 978-1-912523-03-0

For Elizabeth: but only the good bits.

Contents

Introduction   1

For Elizabeth (when my times comes)	7
Curating	8
First Step	11
Wasps	12
Night Skies	13
Breeze	14
This Time	15
Asunder	16
When You Came	18
A Name	19
Leaves	20
Too Late	22
Tolpuddle	23
The Asking Of	24
Seas	25
Lost	26
Crowing	27
Away	28
Dredged Up	30
That Song	31
Memory	32
Standing Stones	33
Going On	34
Tick	35
Hurricane	36
Fen Causeway	37
Darkness Coming Through	39

Watching Distance	40
Silence	41
Silence Again	42
Theft	43
Advice to the Young	44
Can't	45
Me	46
Chances	47
Thinking	48
Storm	49
Costs	50
Stories	51
New Purpose	53
Trespass	55
A Certain Place	57
That Imagination	58
Come Again	60
Accounting	62
Burnt	64
Picture	66
Going to Hell	67
Awakening	68
Keeper	69
Malcolm	70
Baldon	72
Steven King (3)	74

Introduction

My grandmother once said of me that I was neither a glass empty nor a glass full sort of boy. Rather, I just smashed the glass. My father had a different take though with the same intent, gleefully telling everyone (including the Vice-Chancellor at my inaugural lecture after I had first been promoted to Professor) that I was sixty when I was six. They both constructed me as a serious boy with a remarkable capacity for being professionally miserable. There was justification, of course, for both the attitude and misery. I was someone who never really fitted in. The farming life that could have been – should have been – was a future prised away by a grasping Oxford college that raised the rent on the family farm by 200% in a single year. This, my parents' divorce, and an all too powerful sojourn on council estates have shaped me. I am something more than a pessimist. Perhaps I need my own label.

Yet, and despite this personality ambiguity, I never seemed to have much trouble 'falling into' relationships. Some were little more than fleeting encounters; others grew or were grown into something more substantial. Few of them ended well or in a process of conscious uncoupling. Sometimes this was my fault. I am largely unchanging, tied to traditions, rituals and beliefs, and so those that came in thinking I could be shaped soon found themselves walking through tar. But much more often, fault was shaded. My mother largely spat out recrimination on the women (she invariably called them 'gurls'): 'You're just too nice', she'd say. That is, she felt I did too much, paid too many bills, did not demand enough. It was more than that, however, even if in some cases her diagnosis was spot on. For convenience, protection, evasion and because it is 'just me', I believe everything: what people tell me, their answers to my questions, their reactions and stated feelings. And I do not go further. The alternative would be to question, seek meaning, to construct scenarios from glances or hints. This is not how I have wanted to live my life, but the attitude has consequences.

Take for instance the person I met at an academic conference early in my career. She told me that she was separated from her husband and was in the process of divorcing him. I believed her – there was certainly no wedding ring or any mark where one had recently been – and notwithstanding some physical distance between us we took up as a couple. This moved from hotel meets to her visiting my house in the north. Eventually I was invited, at unpredictable intervals, to stay with her in a very nice house. Much was spoken (by her) about pasts, presents and futures. Then on one visit, as I was getting ready to leave, something suddenly nagged. A voice, that of the sage General you will hear elsewhere in this volume, called me upstairs. I opened up a large cupboard and out tumbled the evidence of her husband, carefully stashed away the moment he had left for his boys' weekend and ready to be just as carefully replaced again when I had gone. There was no separation, divorce or even uncoupling. Merely a lie. We did not speak again, though she is here in my poems if you can find her.

Or perhaps another tale, this time of someone from university days. We drifted together when we were both at an ending. It was slow burn (from my point of view) but we visited her parents often as she was very close to them. We went yet again to see the parents. When I arrived, everyone was dressed in suits. There were flowers and some air of celebration. Clearly I had forgotten a major birthday, which would be par for the course. Until, that is, people started coming up to congratulate me and to say how much they were looking forward to the ceremony. My girlfriend had organised our wedding without asking, hinting or telling. I was the only person who did not know. So I went upstairs to a bedroom – 'to change'; I had brought a suit for an assumed dinner out – climbed through the window and drove away as fast as those country roads would allow.

I could (unfortunately) go on. Each of those failed journeys left a mark as they do for everyone. In some cases, I remain resentful and angry even after the passage of years. Mostly, though, I am reflective, a mood sharpened by finding someone I was certainly meant to be with. For this reason, I struggled with the title of my volume. It started as 'On Hope and Despair', morphing into 'On Love and Hate' and then, after a discussion with my friend Keith Snell, into 'On Chance' or 'On Chance Encounters'. Finally, though, the title became the one you are now reading: 'On Love and Loss'. This is in part because some of those people were lost. For instance, my first 'real' relationship as a boy was with a much older woman. She was killed in her car when on the way to give me a birthday present. But all fizzled or failed relationships leave an imprint of loss, and that (alongside hope for the future) is what you see in these poems.

Whether I was this philosophical at the time I cannot fully remember. But I think that I did bounce back relatively quickly. This position might be contrasted with what I can see around me amongst a younger generation. The breakdown of fleeting and minor relationships seems prone to being magnified into crisis, mental breakdown and reverse. Something of resilience has been lost and absence of connection and commitment is growing fast. A sense that lives inevitably break apart, and that clawing back is natural and healthy, disappears. Speaking about anxiety, likely the leitmotif of the 2020s, is a weed-ridden substitute for speaking of love and loss. Perhaps the young should turn to poetry rather than counselling services, or at least they could have if the lunatic liberal elites had not just tried to cancel it in the curriculum.

As I have grown out and up I see more magic, more hope perhaps, than I could have done at six or likely will at sixty. To find someone is to change, even if that change is barely perceptible in my histories. To keep a relationship going requires a curious mix of luck, design and avoidance. To lose, though, is not to collapse but to learn and start a new conversation. I have had many conversations, perhaps too many, and my father continues to regale the world with his story. He forgets, of course, that I am pretty close to sixty and either his words will soon lose their currency or (since he is some decades older than me even if he protests the contrary) he might lose the breath to convey them. But he still has breath, notwithstanding the best efforts of the NHS, and so I wonder what he might say just now, surveying Elizabeth and me? Perhaps that, despite my being composed of some strange façade of contradictions, despite my being ever so slightly odd, hopefulness won out. Or perhaps he would echo a neighbour who recently noted that, despite being a curious mixture of introvert with extrovert tendencies, Steve turned out alright.

STEVEN KING
JANUARY 2021

ON LOVE AND LOSS

For Elizabeth (when my times comes)

On this little sojourn, I
forgot to take the exit
to interesting, and yet you
found me just the same.

I was an odd-looking bag
of humanity, perhaps not
even that, and you puzzled
me back together, my own Morse.

We sang a song nigh two
miles long. 'Scarborough
Fair' in our own drastic and
hapless unmelodic tune.

You called the moon to
account for making us look
like a pair of moderns, and
we struck the stars together.

But I have outrun the span
of life allotted to me by our
fortune teller. As I leave,
let me tell you this at last:

The heart has many dwelling
places but only a single home.

How fast can a soul travel
to meet with you again?

Curating

You plucked me from
obscurity so that I could
stand, still life, in your
museum of misfits.

And I did well, paddling
through the clutter of
each day, powered by
gold and good intentions.

I did ask: what is the
purpose here? But you were
not for the telling and I,
perhaps, not for the listening.

And so we troubled along
in this injured place where
the imperfects and the
crippled storytellers come.

But there *was* a plan, and I was
not so innocently travestied.
It was this: I was to be your ring
master in the bleak little circus.

To confect and direct those
collected shadows in the making
of an entertainment, one to speak
of great substance and control.

And then you stepped beyond
your careful mark, that crafted
boundary placed by caution so
as to shift the note to blameless.

I learnt that you planned on my
being nobody, just another
nameless statue in your heroic
collection of odds and otherness.

That was long ago, half a lifetime
of glacial distance. But now…
do you recognise me, hidden
in this distant and cold persona?

Surely you must, after all that
passed between us? I see
not, so let me tell my final
words of then once more:

A rotten core cannot be healed.
The rot will grow and deepen,
to weaken the whole until the
slightest breach or stress brings
a spectacular break asunder.

I am back. And for the first trick
of my ringmasterly return, feel
the weight of happenstance as
you crack and crumble away from
those so confident foundations.

And now the parts are moving.
They will harry you to their worst.

First Step

If the world lies in pieces
you should make it anew,
for there is a chance of miracles
and the greatest of them is you.

So when things break or tumble and
the plasters will just not hold fast,
stand and watch the pieces fall
until the you of you arrives at last.

Wasps

The wasp held fast to the fence
in that vertical sort of way,
scraping in almost silence.

Here was the making of a nest,
full of stings and venom.

After some time, when the
scraping beak was full, our
wasp lifted to the wind and
took determined flight, a
dash of yellow and black
across a face of pitchy brown.

And you came to mind.

For you are out there,
somewhere, in your nest of
paper and poison with the
drones gathering treasure in.

Until some stray spark brings a
fiery end to that stinging life.

Strike…

Night Skies

You tested the character of the night.
It cloaked you as if a first encounter.
In the distance, a clock ticked backwards
but we could not see for the hearing.
We talked ourselves to silence, and
as the stars struggled through the
mooning canvas we picked them with
tweezered fingers. You held a light of old
and wished your whole story told.

Now you have done your laborious part,
and we have reached an end, I could
give your whole pedigree. But no.
Let us push aside the rubs of the world,
and just remember that darkening moment.

Breeze

I tried to be the breeze,
wrapping you all around.
But was I that in fact, or just
some tepid act of imitation?

You must take your favourite
spot, and judge anew.
I cannot account for our
recent final transactions.

You have gained pockets
full of gold and a self
freighted with life's treasure.

But what of the breeze and
the stories that it told? The
hope of moving on that it
offered with every starting?

You reject it.
Our time is spent.
And the till is empty.

So as my breeze
softens, dies to
some anaemic wheeze,
just remember this:

A heavy boat needs sail, and
flounders when the wind dies away.

This Time

Today is not a dying day,
though once it might have been.

Today is not a dying day,
no matter how it seems.

No.

Today is a living day,
and now's the time to dream.

Asunder

I heard
the word
and drank
it in,
tho' its
sentiment was
so deathly
thin.
And now
let me
give back
somehow
this little
consolation:
there is
at last
no holding
fast,
for we
go our
different ways
and are
split as by axe.
Goodbye my
shadow so
life-long.
Now it's
here I
must be
gone.

We'll meet
some time
when life
is fine
and our
little loathings
are put
to rest.

When You Came

You picked the moon and
wrapped it all away.

You shouted at the stars
and breathed their paling light.

You teased the sun to show,
and dawned so gently in its arms.

You hurried the clouds along
with your song of the wind.

You stood in that twilight
up against the falling glow,
and I knew then that a woman
of command had come.

A Name

I am a man who's lost his name.
I've spent too long playing this game.
Let me go now for all that I've done,
so that a time of ending can come.

Or, perhaps, you'll hold on tight and
promise again to make it right? But you
know there's no material for the making
when you've spent it all on faking.

Give me back my name.
Forget the playing of this game.
And then we can both be free,
to move on, as wood becomes tree.

Release me.

Leaves

There was that certain chill
that only a Cambridge autumn
can deliver. Flaming red and
hark-me-back-to-summer yellow
had faded then to brown, a
deep wade-in-me carpet of the
fallen and decayed along this
avenue of smooth-barked giants.

And, in a most un-Cambridge-like
moment, there was nobody.
Except us.

Was it I who first parked my
shrivelled maturity and took some
kicking, scraping steps into the
knee-deep of crisp and crisping
leaves? Or was it you, drawn in
by the unfolding story to let go?

No matter, for we were heaving
our path, knee after knee,
with nothing of feet to see.
Behind us, just a stolen glance note,
lay our signal trail, straight and true.
And we did not speak in case the
speaking of it should make the air
grow colder still.

But we looked and took in the smell,
scuffing purposively as if set in a spell.
Just for these moments, the world
was framed, stood as it was meant to be.
It could not last, could not hold fast this
colour of a water colour. Soon enough
those strange imitation Americans
came to trample what could have been
their magical scene.

We smiled, and sank back into
that memory of trees and leaves
and the grasping perfume of falling.
You remember this.
I know you do.

Let us return this Cambridge way,
and claim a scene that is rightly
ours. It's time to go a-scampering
on some Cambridge sort of day.

Too Late

The doing of making do
tortured the creative you.

Tho' we did our turn, the
we of us was slowly lost.

I tried my trying best
as wonted the eldest there.

But the I of me was consumed
and vanish'd. You did this.

Tolpuddle

Somewhere along that
Dorset mile, you might
have seen it. Had you
been in looking mind.

That sequestered place
where resisting words
can gather like threads of
mist, to be calmed into
something more substantial.

A rumour perhaps or
some certain movement
to be sprung upon those
favoured lives that keep
a poor man in his place.

Stop now on your light-
footed progress and
hear that silence. For
men and not just words
died here that you might
have your freedoms.

The Asking Of

You asked me,
but I did not listen.

You asked me this,
but I did not care.

You asked me this question,
but I could not answer.

You asked me this question anew:
what will you be in your time?

That time is easing,
as tree returns to wood, and now
we know that my life has
come to no good.

Seas

The sea pushed me away, its
dappling shallows flowing unclaimed.
Ariel, sighing in the tree tops, came
into silence, and all was well with
my annual growlings. Perhaps if you
listen to the song of the spray,
carried so gently into your way,
my voice will tell of this: you
wrote a lovely storyline and hung it
round my neck.

Lost

Can you tell me the way?
Think carefully.
For if you can, the chance is yours.
Should you call it wrong, I will
fall into some spiked trap and
my blood will negotiate away.

I *must* be in my
finding space
and in this place
let me confess:
I had the chance
of often but
turned my
face away.

Crowing

The wind is coldening and
I must go from this place.
But what a thing I have seen.

A clattering, chattering of
crows just gathered me
in, feather by feather.

These black masters of
their own time acted
their foolery and called
this man to account.

Now the assassins have gone
to feather, probing this
place of land and reeds,
issuing their defixio.

Can you hear that chorus
of hoarse and dusking voices?
Luck-breeders have come to
roost by the authority of
the night and to talk to
the moon, folding me out.

I must go and you with me.

Away

I wanted away,
but the way was
not for yielding
to some vague
and slavish wish
made in the rush
and hush of a
night drawn out.

And so I am stuck
like some tubbed
tree with the roots
grown out, clinging
with tenacity in a
place I can't belong.

The cutting of this
root, so entwined
with you, will cause
harm to more than
me, but I cannot
help this maudlin
outcome. Nor would
you want me to.
For your away came
early and its winding
path has taken you far.

Now, as you wander
up our steepening
hill clothed in hedgerows,
you hope to hear some
voice – my voice –
signalling you in.

I am sorry to disappoint.
For I want away,
though it might be
death should that tap
root not take again.

Dredged Up

When they chattered their
inanities, you piped up
'I'm not fond of hearing a
goose fart' and the preen
was soon passing by.

When they talked of this
and that machine, you
looked askance and told
them it was time they got
their blisters honourably.

When they gossiped
just in reluctant hearing,
you issued forewarning
that those who bring
will also likely carry.

You were of no period
and yet of every age.
And as I pass into the
dark shade of the unknown
without you, know this:

When my dry bones shake
at last, we shall meet again.

That Song

Your mournful song,
stretches decades long.
Forever Autumn turned
to winter soonest
when your car crumpled
on that last of elms.
A birthday record survived.
Your life died.

Memory

My name holds fast
onto this place though
centuries have past.

I am an old soul, not so
easily flushed away
by these noisy tides.

How many times has me
been reshuffled in
mingled magnificence?

Why, many. And in that
comfort of knowing,
let me offer this advice.

Put aside that sharp
chatter and the critical
pickety-pick. Rush yourself
out of habit. For it is a
ghostly thing that holds
your hand and speaks of
something better.

Standing Stones

It is standing in another place,
so why do you come creeping
here?

I have less breath than my
years ago, and so what
would you have me rattle?

Well this is a thing.

Silence, embodied all
around with your face.
What am I to make of it?

Come, stand not bark-like,
clinging to some unseen,
unyielding core.

Please. You look at me
with that mild serenity,
understanding but not
somehow engaged.

Speak. Why have you come?
It is standing in another
place, where you and I
will be one. Is that not enough?

No, I see not.
It is standing in
another place.
A grave, a mound
and I am done.

Going On

The door has closed its close.
The window has shuttered shut.
The lock has turned its stiffest turn.
The floorboards have creaked their creak.

I knew you would come for me,
and what the consequence might be.
So pour out the stars into my bowl of
wishes and I will drink them down.

What will they say of me then,
when I wear that magical crown?

Tick

There was a chance.
Once.
That I could hitch a
ride on some fleeting dream.

There was a hope.
Once.
That I could be better
than my father's intent.

There was a desire.
Once.
To throttle the odds and
make some unlikely ascent.

But now the clock ticks
to certainty, and what have
I become with you?

Hurricane

I was the chance of your chance encounter.

You stood on that wretched morning
between a wish and its coming
and we grew to a happy sort.
But the charlatan came to bear.
His waterfall words drowned
out the good sense that had
served you well of old, and
you succumbed to his
Cromwellian wheeze. But
you did not grasp the story.
For once you give the charlatan
power it never does return. You
were but the fleeting fibre
in his tissue of deceptions,
and now that all is out
it is too late for that brittle regret.
The sharpening winds of life-fall
will carry you along and drown
out your saddest song.

Fen Causeway

The mists of everyday
early morning
clung stubbornly
against a rising sun
on this Cambridge lung.

We talked and walked
as if there was no work
to set us straight. And
those cows looked in
that querysome way
that only Cambridge
cows can look. Everybody
was somebody here
except perhaps us.

One of them could not
resist, hulking like
a lecherous don
towards us, each misty
hoofing step in turn.

Until he stood, not
much resembling a window,
and called his Cambridge
call. In this fen moment
you bent and blew into
his nose, a primal act
in this ancient space.

For your cheek you
got a slap of some
enormous dark tongue.
Eating now but edible
soonest, pushing up
your face. How the
newsman caught this
on his lens for the
Cambridge Evening News
we will never know, for
we never saw that busy
Pecksniffian.

But catch he did, a
gift into his lap, thrown
in a most unknowing
way. Do you remember this,
and that succeeding kiss?
Or is this picture now
consigned, as I, to some
meddlesome back story?

Darkness Coming Through

I dream of a place unseen
and go to a place unbidden,
as the summer rolls from
side to side. But my imagination
is as of wood, unyielding
and yet fine grained.

There never was a path
that I could follow to an end,
and so I am called back to
this reality.

That remarkable dark thing
stands in the shadows
waiting for me to walk the
corner; it will jump on my
back and twist me to contortion.

When it has had its way, and
I am a shell of anxious, perhaps
the dreams will fill me up
like sand and give me that
stodgy clumping foundation.

There is hope.

Perhaps.

Watching Distance

You were changed by change
but I stood still through all.

And now we are parted at last
I wish that I had caught your tail.

For as you walk into that certain
distance, I have no stepping
stones to guide me through.

I am to be alone, absent from
a scene where I should have
been the principal.

Silence

I told the times and
waited for your applause,
but there was only silence.
And I suffered.

When nothing was to be had,
you took it nonetheless.
And I suffered.

When everything was to be gained,
you threw it casually away.
And I suffered.

When everything was to be lost,
you embraced the losing of.
And I suffered.

When your last request fell short,
you took yourself to distance.
And I suffered.

And I suffer still, for my
everything was ripped apart,
and fashioned again in
a broken guise. My
shining gold slipped out, and
only my sadness was left.
You meant this.

Silence Again

When nothing was to be had
you took it nonetheless.
And I suffered.

When everything was to be
gained, you threw it casually away.
And I suffered.

When everything was to be lost
you embraced the losing of.
And I suffered.

When your last request was refused
you took yourself to distance.
And I suffered.

And I suffer still.

For my everything was ripped
apart and fashioned again
in a broken mould.
My shining gold tipped
out and only my darkness
was left to torment me.

You did this.

Theft

That luck you gathered in
which should have been my
own. Did it do you good, as
it would have done for me?
No matter. Our time has
dripped away under your
fleeting sort of care. A
drawing wind takes up
my ash and I am broken
from a lonely corpus.

You scratched out this life.
But I will be around again.
For I am the thunderstorm,
and there's lightning in this pen.

Advice to the Young

Wait.

Before you speak of feeling anxious,
do not just accept the forecast
and talk yourself to damage.
Write a history of doing, not
of fearing to do.

That remarkable thing stands
in the shadows, waiting for its
happenchance.

To what do I refer, you ask?
Well, of hope and a certain love
of you. So tip out the stars
and fuse them with a wish
that you might escape from this.

Can't

I can't see.
But I know the chance has gone.

I can't smell.
But I know your perfume fades.

I can't hear.
But I know your chatter falls.

I can't be.
But I know escape has closed.

I can't feel.
But you know that.
Because you walked away.

Me

I wrote myself today
but no one noticed.

Such brilliant words slumped
to the table, unheard
except in my imagination.

And tomorrow, when
I look into that telling
mirror, I will wish that
you were not me.

Chances

You arrived with circumstance
that demanded a solid hearing.

So, come, friend, now that we
are met: 'What do you carry?'

Why say you 'a sack of wasted
chances; perhaps you'll oblige
by looking in?'

Now here is a sight to see, turning
over the splinters of what could
have been, piece by blasted piece.

'How came you by these?' I ask.
'Well,' say you,

'I am a gatherer, paying my coin
for these lost stories and calling
in the interest, piece by wretched
piece. And how they pay and
squirm in the dead darkness, when
the cost grows sullen and weighty.'

Thinking

I cannot join you in
the making of a vanity
unless you pull me
over the narrows.

But do.
I am a friendly
place where you
might meet a
fleeting whisper
and say, at last,
I see.

For when the broken
is mended and the
fallen is righted anew,
I can capture a future
with the slightest signal
from you.

Storm

This fragment of darkness
sits atop my soul, multiplying
as if planted in some
tenacious kind of earth.

So while the man in flesh
might not be merged and lost,
that sempiternal signal of
evil twists and turns as some
substantial shadow, blown
by the blackest wind.

Beware lest I should draw
you in, for you will see
only innumerable drops of
rain until the darkest storm
is upon you.

Should this happen, I
will observe and drink in
your suffering from my
watching chamber.

And I will be happy.

Costs

There was a price
There was a price
And the paying of it's here.

You knew
You knew
Those times ago
That the price was clear.

Turn back now
Turn back now
For it's a price to fear.

Run.

You have a chance.

I speak of somehow
And ask you to pick up
The hearing of it.

Take hold and fashion
This somehow into a
Different sort of star.

Or stay,

And die with me today.

Stories

Five stories ago
an old wish came true
and me became you.

Four stories ago
when you lost me,
what was I to think?
Or to say, in a world
that was not for
the listening of?

Three stories ago,
the pain rose
as of beech smoke,
a thousand delicate
tendrils wrapping me
well in. But I had not
planned on you,
nor that timely rescue
and the hand offered
to this strange creature.

Two stories ago,
I wished I'd embraced
that little challenge
and turned out my
habit to graze on
some new pasture
or rich forest floor.

In the now, when
these brittle leaves
rise up under the suck
of the wind, you come
through. We have reached
a peaceable settlement
at last.

New Purpose

And so I arrived,
but past the caring of it.

You told me his secret
that I might stir it
into a scandal.

I enjoyed that
little delicacy
and thanked you
for its confection.

But you misunderstand
me.

When the darkness comes
I should be of the dark,
but I am not evil
and I will not fit your legacy.

The gossiping of secrets is a
mortal game.

Now comes a night of raging.
And of danger.

This ending light will
be the last to drink in.
You have met your time.
Die, and hope that
some future prospector
takes hold of your
shrivelled piece of
humanity and resurrects
you to the world.

Trespass

Private.
Stay out.
Yes, you.

Or perhaps not.
Come.
Let us to
our gossip wend.

Tell me all
that I may
better weave my
web of deception.

Come.

Before the sun
falls down and
the clock strikes
to forgetting time,
tell me all.

Then I'll
be the piper,
calling the price
to pay. And
I'll enjoy the
misery, creeping
from day to day.

For I am bad
of heart and
deed.

Private.
Stay Out.

Unless, unless.

You've a mouth
full of poison
in return for
pockets full
of silver.

A Certain Place

The hedgerows were anoise
ahead of my intruding footfall.
A mist hung, almost edible, and
somewhere in that distance a
group of talkers floated their
words on matchsticks.

Their gossip was bodied up
for all to see
and some of that walking
gossip told of me.

What should I have done?
Stand, as if frozen
in some outrageous posture?
Lifted my chin from its
melancholy rut and walked
alone with pride?

Or kill, with that delicate
satisfaction?

I was found to want,
not to be wanting.
But what is the conclusion
to this story?

That Imagination

General George Slender
joined me on the stairs
and I talked to him of strategy,
of bravery, and of fighting bears.

His advice to me was clear:
'Speak not of this encounter
lest they think you mad
and lock you up in fear.'

But some further sage advice
struck this boy of eight:
'For every good intention
expect to pay a price.'

'Pull in your horizons, boy,
and look into yourself.
Keep a part of you wrapped
up, impervious to joy.'

'When the bad times come,
you'll thank me for these words,
for you can unwrap that fragment
and rely on its foundation.'

'Here is the material to encase,
so busy your hands and
make that parcel incognito.
Come, don't let it waste.'

'Now hide the shard away,
young boy, and think of it
no more. Just remember me
and the need of it one day.'

General George Slender
joined me on the stairs,
but in my adult mind, he
was not truly there.

Or, perhaps, my memory
sticks in tar and gum.

'Who're you talking to?'
'No one.'
'But you wus, I heard
someone talking back.'

General George Slender
joined me on the stairs,
and in my lowest newness
he fades into view afresh.

Come Again

You are a piece of bad history.
And you are a bad historian.

The stories that you told,
those sad stories of old,
took me in and spun me round.

I wanted to ink you for
eternity under the skin.
My life was sheet-thin
and threadbare in that
romantic sort of way.

You knew, and plucked
advantage where there
should have been none.

But I was not your
everything when the men
came to take us away.

No, I was that certain
sacrifice: necessary, planned,
unfortunate perhaps,
but something forgiven
and forgotten.

Until now.

I am back and there is
a price to pay:

The wood.
The tree.
The soul to see.

And I see yours,
rotten to its core.
I'll take it in payment
and fashion it afresh,
carve out its imperfections
and shape a brand new you.

Accounting

You called me to account.
But I could not.
Or, at least, would not.

I took what I knew
and all too swiftly flew
from this nest of your making.

You called me to account.
But I should not.
Or, at least, ought not.

For if I tell
of what I knew,
of what I knew of you,
what good would
the knowing of it do?

You called me to account.
But I would not.
Or, at least, could not.

For it was that little cheat
that set my feet
for walking all afar.

You called me to account.
But you forgot that
double entry of accounting.
A debit and a credit,
where the debit falls to you.

You called me to account, that
then you might explain or justify.
But too late.

You called me to account.
But I was not for reckoning.
So savour this parting shot.

There is a place where
memories lay at rest.
For those of happiness,
a tomb deep inscribed
by love. For those cut loose
in sadness, a coating of
that certain toxic dust. Enjoy
its breathing. You and yours
are here in that familiar
guise of a rushed bloom
oh so quick to fade.

Burnt

Do not stand in
ashes, as if you were
a smouldering stump.
It is the rarest tree
that can flourish from
its burning roots.

No

Pick up your feet
and tread those ashes
down, that, looking
back, you may see a
certain impression of
the moment you
turned from reverse.

Maybe

If you carry on your
way and walk the ashes
from your soles, leaving
those crazy particles in
your wake, then the fear
that started this existential
fire will yield to bigger steps.

Yes

It is time.
Look at me again.
I am here, as I
have always been,
could you just but
see me.

Jump

You will not be for the
falling and I'll not be
for the fumbling.

Picture

I am that box of shards
for your mosaic.

Lay the grout and tap me in
to your grand design.

And when I am a picture,
ever so slightly ragged, but
fetching nonetheless, I can be
more than ornament and vanity.

A path, say, of Roman intent,
to take us on our way.

What does this make me?
Some mask of submission or an
artefact of glorious puppetry?

No. I have spent so long doing
cartwheels in the winds of
fortune that I want this. To be
made with care and love,
constructed in a different face.

Do this for me, and let the
world sit in its surprise.

Going to Hell

There is a reason
and a reasoning
but I cannot see the way.
I've long since suffered to
silence, as the price to pay.

I was on the verge of
somewhere, but better
never came along.

Rescue there is none, and
none deserved, for I am that
sinner of yesterday and today.

Forgive me a little at least,
that when I hurry from my perch
there is more than nothing to say.

And perhaps you might tell
of me well. Even if I fall to hell?
For midnight is closing fast
at the ending of my say.

Awakening

You had a chance of
eternity but turned its
halter away.

You could, for the
asking, have sat amongst
the moons and listened
to their stillness.

But coulds turned
into nevers. Now
you have come to a
time of wakefulness
but you do not know
what to do with
the waking.

Listen.
What does the stilling
say to you?
Why, that wonder stands
where you cannot see it,
in front of your nose even
as you breathe it in.

Listen.
Let me make this suggestion:
tomorrow need not be
an ending,
as your others have been.

Keeper

I am a keeper of secrets,
as you meant me to be,
and yours is held fast
so that none may see.

You scratched out a life,
but I have come round again.
And now my life's my own,
the keeper demands his fee.

Your memorable offence
stood behind a toothless amiability.
There was a capstone for your
evil, holding decay in check.

But now think on this: you are bad
sinew and bone, and that
accumulating moral sludge will
drag you under soon enough.

We will not meet again, or,
if we do, one of us will be
for the dying of it.

Malcolm

You talked the talk of
secrets and let them
slip out inch by sugary
inch, watching their
intended progress with
those addicted eyes.

And what of them now,
those little morsels of
invitation to harm?

Well, breathe deep, smell
the oily rancour. Take in
that lungful of satisfaction.
And as the last argument
loses its potency, press repeat.

Yet, on the other fist,
just remember this.
No secret stands still,
for good or for ill,
so let me tell of this:

Yours is rising to view,
as salmon to a fly,
and it's too late for
holding tight or crafting
a final appeal. All secrets
come to rest and yours,
long submerged in that
cold repose, will be
delicious in the telling and
crackling in consequence.

Come.
Walk towards me,
that I might visit you with
a poisonous morsel of my own.

Baldon

We talked of better
as if it were a plan,
sitting amongst the stones
and thinking the day along.

Only those small glances
hinted at the newness
that flashed inside,
as if God's forge was pushing
out its sparks into a night sky.

That was a place of mists
where I stole my first kiss.
A place of the dead,
where I grasped a time of living.
A place of sad memories, where
insistent ghosts were laid to rest.

And now, with the world on pause,
we should have a certain cause
to reflect.

For as the rent of life
has racked up, we forget that
Baldon churchyard and its
stones of mystery and thrill.

On reflection then…

Our caperings have come to roost
as we have grown along. Let us
grasp our stars of centuries old
and continue with this (his)story.
Better stands in plain sight,
if we but grasp its hand.

Steven King (3)

When in the flesh
he was bold. A
master of his own
time, but not the
clock which ticked
to finite years.

Yet whisper it:
Pro Vitis Praeteritis
Et Futuris. You have
not seen the last of
him.